MARGARET MORGAN
and
MARY MORGAN PEDLOW

Memorial

A Kid's Guide to
Origami™

Making
ORIGAMI
CHRISTMAS
DECORATIONS
Step by Step

Michael G. LaFosse

The Rosen Publishing Group's
PowerKids Press™
New York

To the memories of Alice Gray and Michael Shall

Published in 2002 by The Rosen Publishing Group, Inc.
29 East 21st Street, New York, NY 10010

First Edition

Book Design: Emily Muschinske
Project Editors: Jennifer Landau, Jason Moring, Jennifer Quasha

Illustration Credits: Michael G. LaFosse

Photographs by Cindy Reiman, background image of paper crane on each page © CORBIS.

LaFosse, Michael G.
Making origami Christmas decorations step by step / by Michael G. LaFosse.
    p. cm. — (Kid's guide to origami)
Includes bibliographical references and index.
  ISBN 0–8239–5874–4 (lib. bdg.)
1. Origami—Juvenile literature. 2. Christmas decorations—Juvenile literature. I. Title. II. Series.
  TT870 .L23422 2002
  736'.982—dc21

                                                    00–013214

Manufactured in the United States of America

Contents

1	What Is Origami?	4
2	Christmas Tree	6
3	Christmas Angel	8
4	Christmas Stars	10
5	Candle Flame	12
6	Christmas Stocking	14
7	Candy Cane Wreath	16
8	Christmas Gift Bow	18
9	Holiday Wreath	20
10	Origami Key	22
	Glossary	23
	Index	24
	Web Sites	24

What Is Origami?

Children in Japan learn the art of paper folding when they are very young. In Japanese, "ori" means folding and "kami" means paper. Japanese people have enjoyed origami for hundreds of years. Today people all over the world practice origami. Origami uses a special language of **symbols**. Once you learn the symbols of origami, you can read an origami book from any country in the world.

All of the origami in this book is folded from square-shaped paper. Most origami paper only has color on one side, but you do not need to buy special "origami" paper. You can make origami using candy wrappers, colorful notepapers, or old magazines. Make sure that the paper is square and is the right size for your project. When you start a project, make sure the paper faces the way the instructions suggest.

Some wonderful origami projects use more than one sheet of paper. These projects are like puzzles. There are several of these designs in this book. By combining several simple folded shapes, you can create many kinds of decorations. The key on page 22 will help you make your origami projects. It also will help explain some of the terms such as <u>mountain fold</u> and <u>valley fold</u> that are used throughout the book.

Christmas Tree

Did you know that the **tradition** of the Christmas tree is only about 500 years old? The Origami Holiday Tree is even newer. The first public display of an origami-decorated tree in the United States was at the American Museum of Natural History, in New York City, almost 30 years ago. The creation of this tree was the idea of Alice Gray, a scientist at the museum who loved origami. With 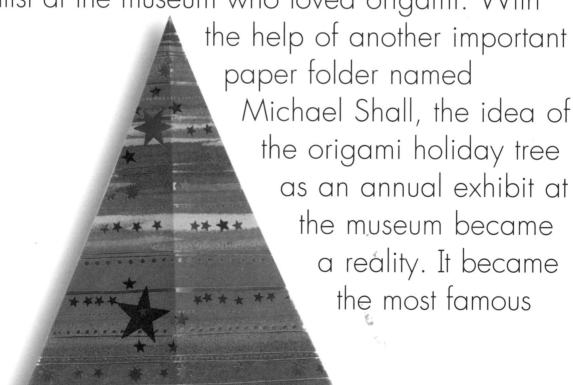 the help of another important paper folder named Michael Shall, the idea of the origami holiday tree as an annual exhibit at the museum became a reality. It became the most famous origami tree of the Christmas season. It continues to inspire people all over the world to create their own origami-decorated trees. Each year, people from all over the world send origami to the **volunteers** at OrigamiUSA for display on the museum's holiday tree. Michael Shall and Alice Gray are two of the founders of OrigamiUSA, an organization devoted to expanding the appreciation of origami.

1

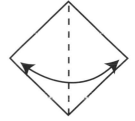

Use a square piece of paper 10 inches (25.4 cm) wide or less. If using gift wrap or origami paper, start with the white side up. Fold in half, corner to corner, and unfold.

2

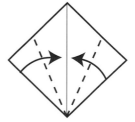

Carefully fold two edges to the crease to make a kite shape.

3

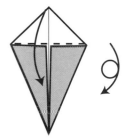

Fold the top corner down and flip the paper over.

4

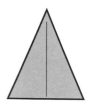

You can glue this tree on a Christmas card or stand it on a tabletop by opening the back flaps. You also can use your Tree in the next project to make a Christmas Angel.

Christmas Angel

Angels played an important part in the Christmas story. An angel delivered the news to the shepherds about the birth of Jesus Christ. It is because of this that an angel sits at the very top of many Christmas trees. If you use 10-inch (25.4-cm) paper, folding an origami Angel for the top of your tree will be easy.

It's fun to use shiny, foil gift wrap to make Angels. You can fold small Angels to make beautiful ornaments for the tree. This origami Angel folds in half, so you also can use it as a Christmas card. Why don't you mail origami Angels to all of your friends this year?

1

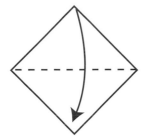

Use two square pieces of paper 10 inches (25.4 cm) wide or less. If you are using gift wrap or origami paper, start with the white side up. Make the Angel's wings by folding a square of paper in half, corner to corner, to form a triangle.

2

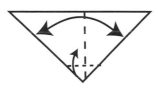

Fold up the bottom corner just a little. Fold the paper in half and then unfold.

3

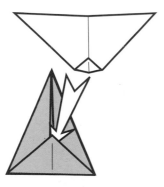

Make the Angel's body from the second piece of paper using the Christmas Tree shape from project number one. Insert the bottom corner of the Angel's wings behind the triangle.

4

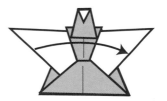

Fold down a little of the top corner, and then fold down the rest of the shape.

5

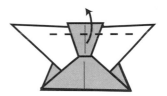

Fold up to make the Angel's head.

6

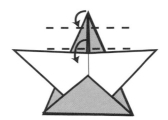

Fold the Angel in half. This Angel can stand all by itself, or you can add a loop of ribbon and make an Angel ornament.

Christmas Stars

The Star of Bethlehem guided the three wise men to the **manger** where baby Jesus was born. A large star often is placed at the top of the Christmas tree to represent the Star of Bethlehem. This Star is made from more than one piece of paper, allowing you to design whatever kind of Star you would like. This project calls for four points, but you also can make a Star with five or six points. Try making a large Star for the top of your Christmas tree.

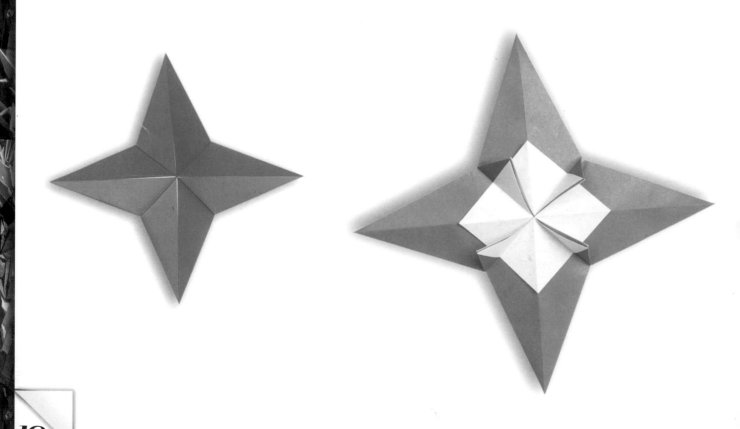

1

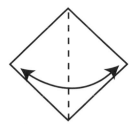

Use four square pieces of paper 6 inches (15.2 cm) wide or less. If you are using gift wrap or origami paper, start with the white side up. Fold in half, corner to corner, and unfold.

2

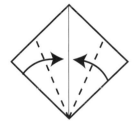

Carefully fold two edges to the creases to make a kite shape.

3

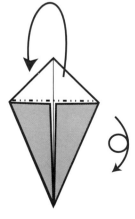

Fold the top corner to the back and flip the paper over.

4

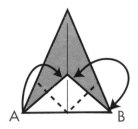

Carefully fold points A and B to the paper point.

5

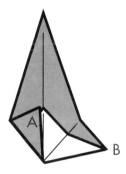

Leave A folded. Unfold B.

6

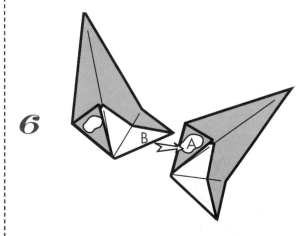

Paste or tape the B corner of one piece to the A corner of another. Continue around until all four points are glued together and make a Star.

Candle Flame

In the **Christian** religion, Christ often is called "the light of the world." The candle flame is a symbol of Christmas because it stands for hope and understanding. The first Christmas trees were decorated with real candles, but today we do not use them because it is too dangerous. Electric lights are much safer because they are less likely to cause a fire. However, you still can add the symbol of the candle flame by making this simple origami Flame. Fold your Candle Flames from foil gift wrap and they will shine brightly on your tree.

1

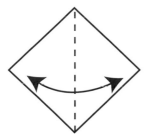

Use a square piece of paper 6 inches (15.2 cm) wide or less. If you are using gift wrap or origami paper, start with the white side up. Fold in half, corner to corner, and unfold.

2

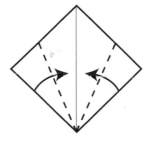

Carefully fold two edges to the crease to make a kite shape.

3

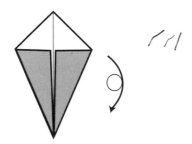

Flip the paper over.

4

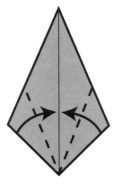

Neatly fold the two short edges into the center.

5

Fold up the bottom corner. Make a <u>mountain fold</u> up the middle and attach a loop of ribbon to make a hanging ornament.

Christmas Stocking

The tradition of hanging up stockings for Santa Claus to fill with treats comes from the Dutch **legend** of Saint Nicholas. On Christmas Eve, Dutch children would leave their wooden shoes near the **hearth** for Saint Nicholas to fill. According to the legend, children who'd been good woke up to find treats in the shoes. Children who'd been bad woke up to find a lump of coal. Today we use stockings, not wooden shoes. If you make an origami stocking from a large piece of gift wrap, you can fill it with treats and give it as a gift. You also can leave it empty on Christmas Eve for Santa to fill!

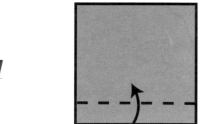

1

Use a square piece of paper 10 inches (25.4 cm) wide or less. If you are using gift wrap or origami paper, start with the colored side up. Fold up the bottom edge.

2

Turn the paper over, and rotate it from the bottom to the top.

3

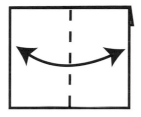

Fold it in half and unfold.

4

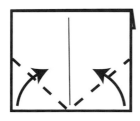

Fold in the two bottom corners to make a point.

5

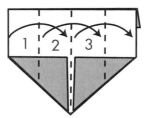

From the left side, fold the paper over three times.

6

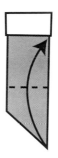

Fold up the bottom point so it touches the white paper.

7

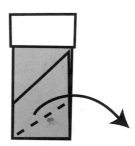

Fold down the top half of the point to make the foot.

Candy Cane Wreath

Jesus Christ often is pictured as a shepherd and is sometimes called "the shepherd of man." The candy cane, which is the same shape as a shepherd's **staff**, stands for Jesus' staff. Also, if you turn a candy cane upside down, it looks like the letter J, the first letter in the name Jesus. To make this candy-cane-colored Wreath, try to use real origami paper or gift wrap that is a solid red on one side and white on the other. You need eight pieces of square paper for this project.

1

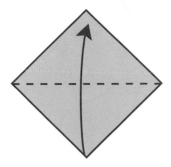

Use a square piece of paper 6 inches (15.2 cm) wide or less. If you are using gift wrap or origami paper, start with the colored side up. Fold in half, corner to corner, to make a triangle.

2

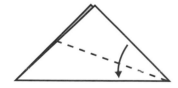

Fold the right side top edge down. Carefully fold so that the edges match.

3

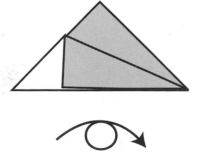

Turn the paper over, left to right.

4

Fold the bottom left corner to the top corner.

5

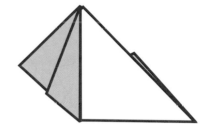

Now you have a finished puzzle piece. Make seven more puzzle pieces by repeating steps 1 through 4 seven times.

6

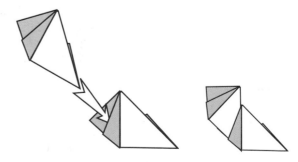

Fit all eight pieces snugly together to make a wreath. Use small Wreaths to decorate gift cards and packages, and place a large one in a window or on your front door.

Christmas Gift Bow

Even with colorful wrapping paper, a package without a bow looks plain. This Bow is neat because it stands out like a shining star. These origami Bows have a lot of folds, but they are quick and easy to make. You can make big Bows for big packages and small Bows for small packages.

You can use any kind of paper to make these Bows, and there are always plenty of leftover gift wrap scraps after all the presents are wrapped. Cut these scraps into squares and make Bows to match the gifts that you wrapped!

1

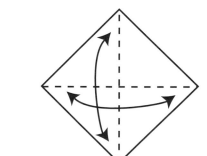

Use a square piece of paper 8 inches (20.3 cm) wide or less. If you are using gift wrap or origami paper, start with the white side up. Fold in half each way, corner to corner, to make crossing creases. Unfold.

2

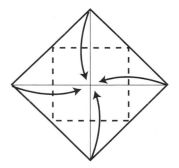

Fold in all four corners to meet in the middle.

3

Fold the four new corners to the middle.

4

Turn the paper over.

5

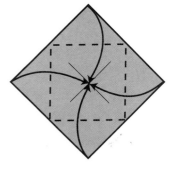

Fold the four corners to the middle again.

6

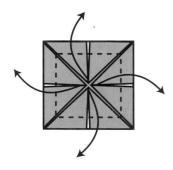

Neatly fold a little of each corner to make an eight-pointed star.

7

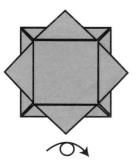

Turn the paper over.

8

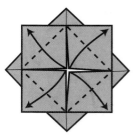

Fold the middle corners out to open the Bow. You should have eight points in the middle of the Bow.

Holiday Wreath

This fancy origami Wreath is a great Christmas decoration to put on your front door or window. You also can make smaller ones to put on a table. Using glue will help hold the biggest Wreaths together. You can make this Wreath using one or two colors. Like the Candy Cane Wreath, this is also like a puzzle with many pieces. You will need 10 pieces of paper to complete this project.

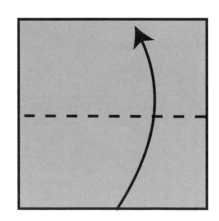

1

Use a square piece of paper 6 inches (15.2 cm) wide or less. If you are using gift wrap or origami paper, start with the colored side up. Fold it in half, bottom edge to top.

2

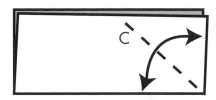

Carefully fold down the right-side short edge of paper to line up with the bottom edge. Unfold.

3

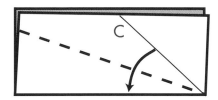

Neatly line up the C crease with the bottom edge.

4

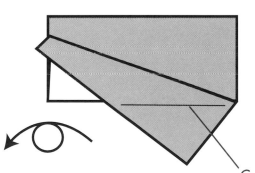

Turn the paper over, left to right.

5

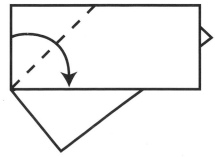

Fold the short, left edge down and line it up with the long, folded edge.

6

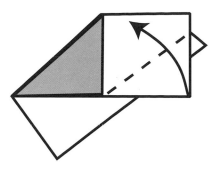

Fold up the right corner. This is the "pocket."

7

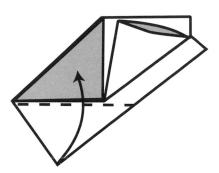

Fold up the bottom corner. Now you have a finished "leaf" for your Wreath.

8

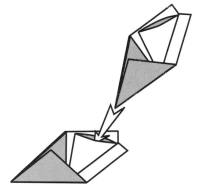

Make nine more pieces like this, and fit each pointed end in a pocket.

9

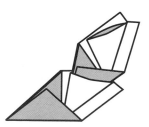

The pieces should fit together to look like the picture above.

Origami Key

1. MOUNTAIN FOLD

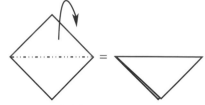

mountain-fold line

To make a mountain fold, hold the paper so the bottom (white) side is facing up. Fold the top corner back (away from you) to meet the bottom corner.

2. VALLEY FOLD

 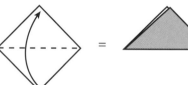

valley-fold line

To make a valley fold, hold the paper so the white side is facing up. Fold the bottom corner up to meet the top corner.

3. TURN OVER

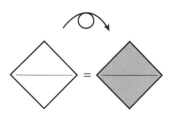

4. ROTATE

 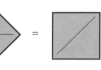

5. MOVE or PUSH

6. CUT

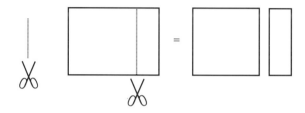

7. FOLD and UNFOLD

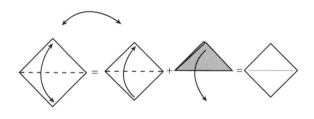

8. DIRECTION ARROW

Glossary

Christian (KRIS-chun) Someone who follows the teachings of Jesus Christ and the Bible.

hearth (HARTH) The floor of a fireplace or the space in front of it.

legend (LEH-jend) A story passed down that many people believe.

manger (MAYN-jur) An open box in a stable used to hold feed for animals.

staff (STAF) A stick, rod, or pole.

symbols (SIM-bulz) Things that stand for or represent something else.

tradition (truh-DIH-shun) A way of doing something that is passed down.

volunteers (vah-luhn-TEERZ) People who offer to help to do something without pay.

Index

A
American Museum of
      Natural History, 6

B
Bow, 18

C
Candle Flame, 12
Candy Cane, 16
Christmas Angel, 8

Christmas Stocking,
      14
Christmas Tree(s), 6,
      8, 10, 12

G
Gray, Alice, 6, 7

J
Japan, 4
Jesus Christ, 8, 12,
      16

O
OrigamiUSA, 7

S
Saint Nicholas, 14
Santa Claus, 14
Shall, Michael, 6, 7
Star of Bethlehem, 10
symbols, 4

W
Wreath, 20

Web Sites

Due to the changing nature of Internet links, PowerKids Press has
developed an online list of Web sites related to the subject of this book.
This site is updated regularly. Please use this link to access the list:
www.powerkidslinks.com/kgo/maorchd/